A SHOE FOR ALL SEASONS

JEFF MACNELLY

A Shoe® for all Seasons

An Owl Book

HOLT, RINEHART AND WINSTON   NEW YORK

Library of Congress Catalog Card Number: 83-80849

ISBN: 0-03-061657-3

First Edition

Designer: Amy Hill
Printed in the United States of America
1 3 5 7 9 10 8 6 4 2

ISBN 0-03-061657-3

Management techniques for the '80's.

Chapter One— How to get the most out of your employees:

Step 1: ...Find your employee.

COMPUTERS HAVE MANY APPLICATIONS TO OUR DAILY LIVES...

SKYLER? CAN YOU NAME SOME WAYS THE COMPUTER HELPS US?

YES, SIR.

THEY HELP US BLAST AWAY GORGON BATTLE CRUISERS.

EEP EEP EEP EEP

WILL THIS GET THERE BY TOMORROW?

NO SWEAT. WE GOT GUARANTEED OVERNIGHT SERVICE.

GOSH...I WONDER HOW THEY DO THAT.

POST OFFICE

HELLO, FEDERAL EXPRESS?

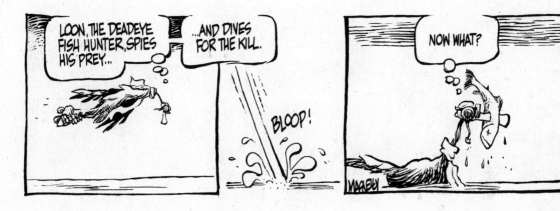

YOU NEVER SIT ON THE FRONT ROW—TOO HIGH A PROFILE. AND THE BACK ROW IS OUT—IT'S TOO OBVIOUS YOU'RE HIDING.

THE BEST SPOT IS DIRECTLY IN THE MIDDLE...

OF MOOSE TIMPKINS' BACK.

WE JUST GOT THIS NOTICE FROM WASHINGTON IN THE MAIL THIS MORNING...

FIRST-CLASS MAIL IS GOING TO 6 CENTS!

THERE MUST BE SOME MISTAKE.

NOPE. IT'S SIGNED BY PRESIDENT EISENHOWER HIMSELF.

SKYLER, I WANT YOU TO TAKE THE ONE COURSE AT SCHOOL THAT WILL HELP YOU IN LATER LIFE...

IT WILL GIVE YOU THE BASIC TOOLS TO DO THINGS LIKE BALANCE YOUR CHECKBOOK... BUDGET YOUR MONEY, HANDLE FINANCES...

HECK, UNCLE COSMO... I'M TAKING MATH ALREADY.

MATH?... I'M TALKING ABOUT CREATIVE WRITING.

NOW, WHEN SKYLER MAKES THE FOUL SHOT, WE GO INTO A FULL-COURT PRESS...

WHAT HAPPENS IF HE MISSES, COACH?

THEN WE HAVE TO CALL A TIME OUT...

SO YOU CAN PRY MY FINGERS FROM HIS SCRAWNY THROAT.

MACNELLY

HE GETS A CRISP PASS AND DRIVES THE LANE...

FOR THE LAY-UP!!

BONK

CLEARLY THIS GAME IS NOT READY FOR THE 4-FOOT POWER FORWARD.

MACNELLY

GADS!! ANOTHER CRUCIAL FOUL SHOT!! I'VE GOT TO MAKE THIS TO PUT THIS GAME INTO OVERTIME...

UMPH!!

NO GOOD!!

ON THE OTHER HAND, I'LL GET HOME IN TIME FOR M.A.S.H.

MACNELLY

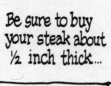

HERE I AM AT THE FOUL LINE AGAIN ... IF I MISS THIS ONE, WE LOSE THE GAME.

BUT I'M COOL ... IT'S ONLY A GAME, AFTER ALL.

THE IMPORTANT THING IS TO DO MY BEST ... BUT STAY REALLY LOOSE.

TIME OUT!

THE OTHER TEAM CALLING TIME, TRYING TO RATTLE ME.

SKYLER!

THERE'S COACH ... CALLING ME OVER TO CALM MY NERVES.

YEAH, COACH?

YOU MISS THIS SHOT, SKYLER, AND YOU'LL NEVER FORGIVE YOURSELF FOR AS LONG AS YOU LIVE ...

NOW THAT I'VE GOT THIS THING IN PERSPECTIVE ...

MACNELLY

The Gallumphing Gourmand. Nutrition:

We should all try to eat well-balanced, regular meals.

These should each include food from the three major food groups:

The Fruit Group...

The Dairy Group...

ICE CREAM

and the Grain Group.

SPOIT

MACNELLY

I'VE HAD IT WITH THAT KLUTZ LOON DELIVERING MY PAPER THROUGH THE LIVING-ROOM WINDOW.

I'M MOVING MY PAPER BOX FAR ENOUGH FROM THE HOUSE SO HE CAN'T POSSIBLY DO ANY DAMAGE.

THERE... JUST IN TIME. HERE HE COMES ON HIS AFTERNOON DROP.

TARGET IN RANGE...

BOMBS AWAY!!

GOOD GRIEF! HE DID IT!!

THUNK

FOOM

CRASH

MACNELLY

I JUST LOVE THIS TIME OF YEAR, SHOE...

THE SNOW AND ICE OF WINTER HAVE MELTED...

REVEALING THE LUSH PROMISE OF YOUNG VEGETATION BENEATH.

AND THE COLORS!! TO SEE COLOR ON THE LANDSCAPE AT LAST! ...AFTER LONG MONTHS OF DREARY GRAY!!

SEE THE NEW GRASS!! THE DAFFODILS POKING UP THROUGH THE SOIL!!

THE BIRDS BACK ON THE BRANCHES!

THE NEW BUDS IN THE TREES...

THE OLD BUDS IN THE ROAD.

MACNELLY

MACNELLY

DID YOU EVER NOTICE THAT BIRDS LOOK LIKE DIFFERENT AIRPLANES?

REALLY?

YEAH. THERE GOES ONE THAT'S A DEAD RINGER FOR A PHANTOM JET.

AND THERE'S THE CONCORDE...

THE OLD BEE GEE RACER!

THE B-1 BOMBER...

AND LOOK OVER THERE!

THE GOODYEAR BLIMP!

MACNELLY

IN THE INTEREST OF BETTER JOURNALISM WE HAVE TO TAKE STOCK OF THE DIRECTION WE'RE TAKING THIS NEWSPAPER.

WE SHOULD BE SETTING A GREAT EXAMPLE FOR OUR CRAFT.

I WANNA MAKE THIS NEWSPAPER BRIGHT... INTELLIGENT!!

A PARAGON OF GOOD TASTE...

A THOUGHTFUL, RESPONSIBLE CIVIC VOICE.

AN URBANE, ERUDITE, INTELLECTUAL JOURNAL THAT DOESN'T TALK DOWN TO THE READER...

BUT CHALLENGES HIS INTELLECTUAL CURIOSITY.

GREAT.

NOW, HOW DO WE GET ANYBODY TO READ IT?

Cincinnati beat the Jets 42-35, Seattle smashed Tampa 27-3, the Giants wriggled past the Eagles 28-27,

Washington blasted Dallas 42-7, the Pats blitzed the Colts 31-3,

Los Angeles frazzled the Dolphins 31-17, the Raiders creamed the 49ers,...

Houston devastated the Saints 51-6, Chicago clobbered Green Bay 27-10, Pittsburgh pulverized the Lions 42-9,

Cleveland annihilated Kansas City 24-0, Buffalo disemboweled Atlanta 31-17, St. Louis discombobulated Denver 10-7, and San Diego....

?

dekrelnificated the Vikings 19-14.

HECK, EVEN SPORTSWRITERS RUN OUT OF VERBS SOMETIMES.

MacNELLY

These new computers we're using in newsrooms these days are certainly wondrous,

but it's not the same for us old veterans of the blue-pencil-and-glue-pot era.

We miss rolling that copy paper into the battered Underwood and pounding out a story.

Now our stuff silently appears in a green glow on this newfangled, electronic screen.
   Sure, it's a lot more efficient,

but it seems pretty darned cold and oddly inhuman to us old geezers who miss the clattering of

CHOMP CHOMP CHOMP
oddly inhuman to us old geezers who miss the clattering of

CHOMP CHOMP CHOMP CHOMP clattering of
I KNEW I COULDN'T GET AWAY WITH THIS.

MACNELLY

Define the following:

Hyperbole

The big game played for the championship of Madison Avenue.

I'LL HAVE THE DUCK.

YESSIR...BUT IT DOES TAKE A BIT LONGER TO FIX.

I WONDER WHY DUCK ALWAYS TAKES SO LONG...

BOY, THE WEEKEND CAN'T COME SOON ENOUGH FOR ME.

I REALLY NEED A BREAK FROM THIS COMPUTER SCREEN.

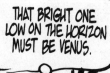

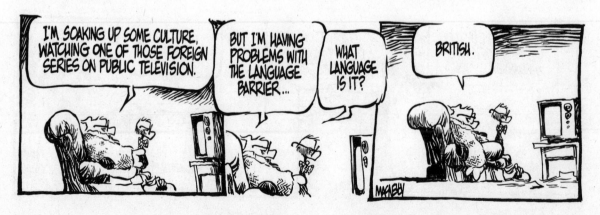

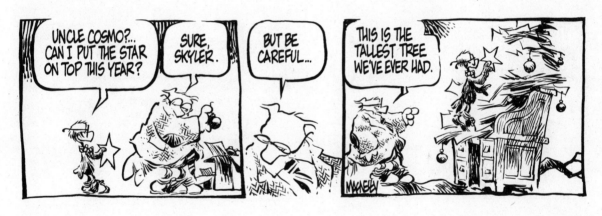